EXTREME SURVIVAL IN THE MILITARY

ROPES & KNOTS FOR SURVIVAL

EXTREME SURVIVAL IN THE MILITARY

EXTREME SURVIVAL IN THE MILITARY

ROPES & KNOTS FOR SURVIVAL

PATRICK WILSON

Introduction by Colonel John T. Carney. Jr., USAF-Ret.
President, Special Operations Warrior Foundation

MASON CREST

Mason Crest
450 Parkway Drive, Suite D
Broomall, PA 19008
www.masoncrest.com

Printed and bound in the United States of America.

10 9 8 7 6 5 4 3 2

Series ISBN: 978-1-4222-3081-7
ISBN: 978-1-4222-3083-1
ebook ISBN: 978-1-4222-8775-0

Cataloging-in-Publication Data on file with the Library of Congress.

Picture Credits
Corbis: 10, 11, 23, 28, 34, 39, 42, 57; **TRH:** 6, 31, 41, 44, 50; **US Dept. of Defense:** 8, 27
Illustrations courtesy of Amber Books and the following supplied by Patrick Mulrey: 13, 14/15, 16/17, 18/19, 20/21, 22, 24/25, 26, 30, 33, 36, 47, 49, 52, 58

ACKNOWLEDGMENT
For authenticating this book, the Publishers would like to thank the Public Affairs Offices of the U.S. Special Operations Command, MacDill AFB, FL.; Army Special Operations Command, Fort Bragg, N.C.; Navy Special Warfare Command, Coronado, CA.; and the Air Force Special Operations Command, Hurlbert Field, FL.

IMPORTANT NOTICE
The survival techniques and information described in this publication are for educational use only. The publisher is not responsible for any direct, indirect, incidental or consequential damages as a result of the uses or misuses of the techniques and information within.

DEDICATION
This book is dedicated to those who perished in the terrorist attacks of September 11, 2001, and to the Special Forces soldiers who continually serve to defend freedom.

CONTENTS

KEY ICONS TO LOOK FOR:

 Text-Dependent Questions: These questions send the reader back to the text for more careful attention to the evidence presented there.

 Words to Understand: These words with their easy-to-understand definitions will increase the reader's understanding of the text, while building vocabulary skills.

 Series Glossary of Key Terms: This back-of-the book glossary contains terminology used throughout this series. Words found here increase the reader's ability to read and comprehend higher-level books and articles in this field.

 Research Projects: Readers are pointed toward areas of further inquiry connected to each chapter. Suggestions are provided for projects that encourage deeper research and analysis.

 Sidebars: This boxed material within the main text allows readers to build knowledge, gain insights, explore possibilities, and broaden their perspectives by weaving together additional information to provide realistic and holistic perspectives.

INTRODUCTION

Elite forces are the tip of Freedom's spear. These small, special units are universally the first to engage, whether on reconnaissance missions into denied territory for larger, conventional forces or in direct action, surgical operations, preemptive strikes, retaliatory action, and hostage rescues. They lead the way in today's war on terrorism, the war on drugs, the war on transnational unrest, and in humanitarian operations as well as nation building. When large scale warfare erupts, they offer theater commanders a wide variety of unique, unconventional options.

Most such units are regionally oriented, acclimated to the culture and conversant in the languages of the areas where they operate. Since they deploy to those areas regularly, often for combined training exercises with indigenous forces, these elite units also serve as peacetime "global scouts" and "diplomacy multipliers," a beacon of hope for the democratic aspirations of oppressed peoples all over the globe.

Elite forces are truly "quiet professionals": their actions speak louder than words. They are self-motivated, self-confident, versatile, seasoned, mature individuals who rely on teamwork more than daring-do. Unfortunately, theirs is dangerous work. Since "Desert One"—the 1980 attempt to rescue hostages from the U.S. embassy in Tehran, for instance—American special operations forces have suffered casualties in real world operations at close to fifteen times the rate of U.S. conventional forces. By the very nature of the challenges which face special operations forces, training for these elite units has proven even more hazardous.

Thus it's with special pride that I join you in saluting the brave men and women who volunteer to serve in and support these magnificent units and who face such difficult challenges ahead.

Colonel John T. Carney, Jr., USAF-Ret.
President, Special Operations Warrior Foundation

To prevent chafing, climbers such as this soldier often use plastic tubing to protect ropes that rub against abrasive surfaces.

WORDS TO UNDERSTAND

improvising: Making something by using whatever is available.

hemp: The fiber that comes from marijuana plants.

Manila hemp: A tough fiber that comes from a plant that's a relative of the banana tree.

sisal: Fiber that comes from the agave plant, a desert plant that also produces a sweet sap used as a sweetener.

synthetic: Manmade; a material that does not come directly from nature.

invaluable: Very useful.

construction: Building.

tendons: The stretchy bands that attach muscles to bones.

THE BASICS OF ROPE CRAFT

Every member of the elite forces has a knowledge of ropes and knots, and how to use them. Soldiers' training is not complete without intense instruction in rope craft and knots; it will serve them well in a survival situation and may even save lives.

Professional-quality ropes can be used in many situations, such as building shelters, assembling packs, making rafts, providing safety devices, **improvising** tools and weapons, and even in first aid. It is important that soldiers practice the knot formations before they find themselves in a situation where they really need them.

What is rope made from?

Traditional rope materials include **hemp**, coconut fiber, **Manila hemp**, and **sisal**, though rope can be made from any material that produces strands of sufficient length and strength.

Many modern ropes are made from nylon and other **synthetic** materials. These ropes are strong, light, and resistant to water, insects, and rot. However, they do have some disadvantages: they can melt if they get too hot, they are slippery when wet, and they can snap due to too much tension.

Troops need to bear all these factors in mind when choosing the type of rope they take with them.

U.S. Marines practice a fast rope descent from a Boeing Sea Knight helicopter onto the landing platform of an assault ship.

Rope terminology

The first part of elite soldiers' training involves getting to know the following words and phrases. These will greatly help them when tying knots.

Bend: used to join two ropes together or to fasten a rope to a ring or loop.

Bight: a bend or U-shaped curve in a rope.

Hitch: used to tie a rope around a timber or post so it will hold.

Knot: the result of tying or fastening ropes or line.

Line: a single thread, string, or cord.

Loop: a fold or doubling of a rope, through which another rope can be passed. A temporary loop is made by a knot or a hitch. A permanent loop is made by a splice.

Overhand loop or turn: made when the running end of the rope passes over the standing part.

A traditional Indian ropemaker makes rope from hemp—the strong fiber extracted from the stalk of the plant *Cannabis salvia*.

Before learning about knots, navy recruits are taught how to estimate the length of a piece of rope, handle long lengths of rope, and form the essential crossing turns that are the basis of many naval knots.

Rope (also called a line): made of strands of fiber twisted or braided together.

Round turn: same as a turn, with the running end leaving the circle in the same general direction as the standing part.

Running end: the free, or working, end of the rope.

Standing end: the balance of the rope, excluding the running end.

 MAKE CONNECTIONS: THE CARE OF ROPES

Ropes need proper care if they are to work effectively for elite troops. The U.S. Rangers follow these guidelines when using ropes for their mountain operations:

- Do not step on rope along the ground.
- Keep away from sharp corners or edges of rocks, which can cut rope.
- Keep rope as dry as possible, and dry it out if it becomes wet to avoid rotting.
- Do not leave rope knotted or tightly stretched longer than necessary, and do not hang it on nails.
- Be careful with nylon rope: the heat generated by rope friction can often melt the fibers.
- Inspect rope regularly for frayed or cut spots, mildew, and rot. If such spots are found, the rope should be whipped (knotted to prevent it from unraveling) on both sides of the bad spots and then cut.

Turn: describes the placing of a rope around a specific object, with the running end continuing in the opposite direction to the standing part.

Underhand turn or loop: made when the running end passes under the standing part.

Choosing the right knot

It is important for a soldier to select the right knot for the right task. The knots listed in this chapter will be **invaluable** in a survival situation. The soldier must practice tying them, and remember to learn to untie them too. Knots must always have the following qualities:

- Easy to tie and untie.
- Easy to tie in the middle of a length of rope.
- Able to be tied when the rope is under tension, and be tied so that the rope will not cut itself when under strain.

Reef knot (Fig A)

This is the same as the square knot (see next page), but can also be tied by making a bight in the end of one rope and feeding the running end of the other rope through and around this bight. The running end of the second rope is threaded from the standing part of the bight. If this action is reversed, the resulting knot will have its

A

Reef knots were traditionally used to tie up sails.

running ends parallel to the standing parts. This type of variation knot is called a "thief knot."

Overhand knot (Fig B)

This knot is of little use on its own, except to make an end-stop on a rope and to prevent the end of a rope from untwisting. It does, however, form a part of many other knots. It is tied by making a loop near the end of the rope and passing the running end through the loop.

Figure-eight (Fig C)

This is used to form a larger knot than would be formed by an overhand knot at the end of a rope. It is used at the end of a rope to prevent the ends from slipping through a fastening or loop in another rope.

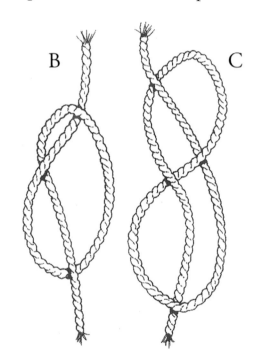

(B) The overhand knot is a multipurpose loop and useful when combined with other knots, while **(C)** the figure-eight knot is commonly used to prevent loose rope slipping through a hole.

To tie this knot, a loop is made in the standing part of the rope, and the running end is then passed around the standing part back over one side of the loop and down through the loop. The running end is then pulled tight to secure the formation.

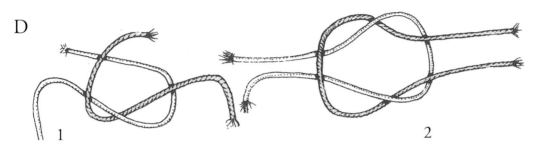

D

1

2

Although a common formation, the square knot is often used incorrectly. Ropes composed of synthetic materials, such as nylon and polyester, are unsuitable for this knot, because they can slip.

Square knot (Fig D)

This is used for tying two ropes of the same thickness together to prevent slippage. A square knot should not be used for ropes of different thickness or for nylon rope, which will slip. This knot is good for first aid because it will lie flat against the patient.

To tie, the running ends of each knot are laid together, although they must be pointing in opposite directions. The running end of one rope is then passed under the standing part of the other rope. Following this, the two running ends are brought up away from the point where they first crossed and are then crossed again (1). Once each running end is parallel to its own standing part, the two ends can be pulled tight (2). It is important that each end is parallel to the standing part of its own rope.

A square knot will draw tighter under strain. It is untied easily by grasping the bends of the two bights and pulling them apart.

Single sheet bend (Fig E)

This is used for tying two ropes of similar size. To tie, the running end of the first rope is passed through a bight in the second one (1). The running

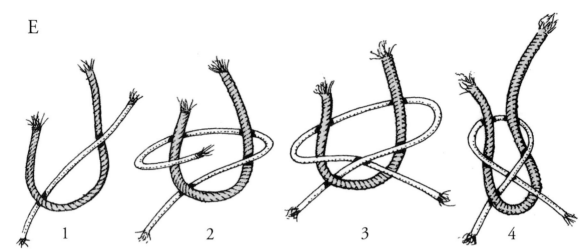

E

1   2   3   4

Step 3 is the most important part of the single sheet bend, because the running end of the second rope must be passed over the front of the knot, at the long end of the loop.

end should continue around both parts of the second rope (2) and back under the first rope (3). The running end can then be pulled tight (4). This knot will draw tight under light loads, but may loosen or slip when the tension is released.

Double sheet bend (Fig F)

This is used for joining together ropes of equal or unequal size. To tie, a variation single sheet bend is tied first (1-5). However, troops do not pull the running end tight. One extra turn is taken around both sides of the bight in the larger rope with the running end of the smaller rope (6). The knot is then tightened (7) and will not slip.

Carrick bend (Fig G)

This is used for heavy loads and for joining together both thin cable or heavy rope. It will not draw tight under a heavy load. To tie, a loop is formed in

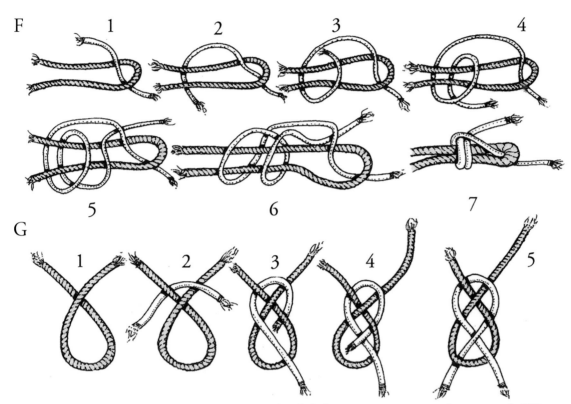

(F) A double sheet bend can be used for joining wet ropes and ropes of different diameter, while a carrick bend (G) is useful for heavier cable that requires extra strength.

one rope (1). The running end of the other rope is passed behind the standing part (2) and in front of the running part of the rope in which the loop has been formed. The running end should then be woven under one side of the loop (3), through the loop over the standing part of its own rope (4), down through the loop and under the remaining side of the loop (5).

Bowline knot (Fig H)

This is used to form a loop in the end of a rope. This loop is extremely easy to untie. To tie, the running end of the rope is passed through the object to be fixed to the bowline, and a loop is formed in the standing

H

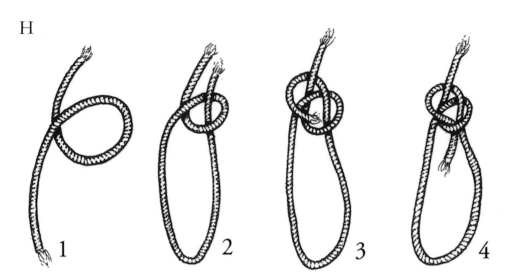

A bowline is ideal for creating loops around the waist, and is used by both climbers and sailors.

part of the rope (1). The running end is then passed through the loop from underneath (2), and around the standing part of the rope (3), and back through the loop from the top (4). The running end passes down through the loop, parallel to the part of the rope coming up through the loop. The knot is then pulled tight to secure.

Triple bowline (Fig I)

This loop is used as a basic sling or boatswain's chair. (This is made by simply adding a hard board with notches for a seat.) In addition, it can be used as a chest harness or as a full harness.

To tie the triple bowline, bend the running end of a line back to approximately 10 feet (3 m) along the standing part (1). The bight is formed as the new running end, and a bowline is tied as described for the bowline knot (2-4). As a sling, the new running end, or loop, is used to support the back and the remaining two loops support the legs.

Bowline on a bight (Fig J)

This is used to form a loop at a point along a rope's length, rather than at the end. It can also be tied at the end of the rope by doubling the rope for a short section. When tying, a doubled portion of the rope is used to form a loop as for a bowline (1). The bight end of the doubled portion is passed through the loop, back down (2), up around the entire length of the knot (3), and tightened (4).

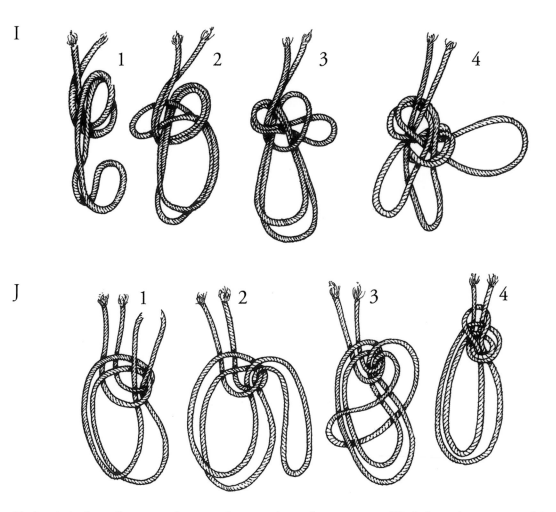

(I) A triple bowline can be used as a chest harness to lift injured personnel to the safety of a helicopter, while the bowline on a bight (J) offers the strength of two loops, which can be adjusted in proportion to each other.

Hitches for every occasion

Hitches are used for attaching ropes to poles, posts, and bars. Some of the most widely used and useful hitches are given below. Troops must learn to master these hitches. They will serve them well in a survival situation.

Half hitch (Fig K)

This is used to tie a rope to a piece of timber or another larger rope. It is not a very secure knot or hitch. To tie, the rope is passed around the timber, bringing the running end around the standing part and back under itself.

The half hitch is simply a circle of rope wrapped around an object.

Timber hitch (Fig L)

This is used for moving heavy timber or poles. To tie, the running end is turned about itself at least another time. These turns must be taken around the running end itself or the knot will not tighten against the pull.

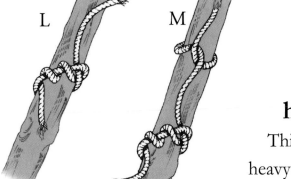

The more a timber hitch is pulled, the tighter it grips.

Timber hitch and half hitch (Fig M)

This is used to get a tighter hold on heavy poles for lifting or dragging. To tie, the running end is passed around the timber and back under the standing part to form a half hitch. A timber hitch is tied further along the timber with the running end. The strain is on the half hitch, but the timber hitch stops it slipping.

Clove hitch (Fig N)

This is used to fasten a rope to a timber, pipe, or post.

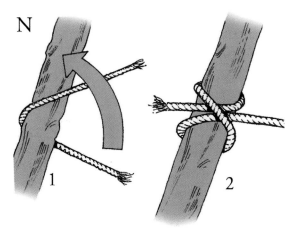

To tie in the center of the rope, two turns are made in the center of the rope close together (1). A soldier then twists them so the two loops lie back-to-back. These two loops are slipped over the timber or pipe to form the knot (2). To tie a clove hitch at the end of the rope, the rope is passed

Composed of two half hitches, the clove hitch is ideal for closing off an enclosed camp or other area.

around the timber in two turns so that the first turn crosses the standing part and the running end comes up under itself on the second turn.

Round turn and two half hitches (Fig O)

To tie, the running end of the rope is passed around the pole in two complete turns. The running end is brought around the standing part and back under itself to make a half hitch. A second half hitch is then made. The running end of the rope should be secured to the standing part.

A simple round turn forms one and a half circles.

Rolling hitch (Fig P)

To tie, the standing part of the rope is placed along the pole opposite to the direction that the pole will be moved (1). Two turns are taken with the running end around the standing part and the pole (2). The standing part of the rope is then reversed so that it is leading off in the direction in which the pole will be moved (3). Following this, two turns are taken with the running end (4). On the second turn around, the running end is passed under the first turn to secure it (5). To make it secure, a half hitch is tied with the standing part of the rope at least one foot (30 cm) along the rolling hitch (6).

Lashings

Lashings are useful in the **construction** of shelters, equipment racks, rafts, and other structures. The most commonly used are the square lash, diagonal lash, and shear lash. They are fairly simple to tie, but elite soldiers will always practice making them.

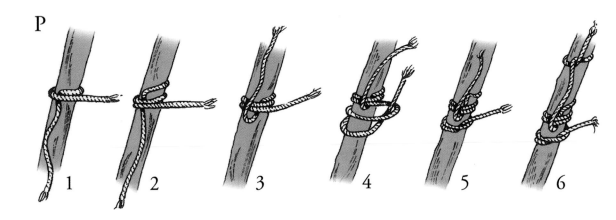

P

1   2   3   4   5   6

A rolling hitch is used to attach a rope to a pole, or to take the strain off another rope. Strain can be applied in one direction only.

Rope climbing builds upper body strength, coordination, and agility. U.S. Marines (above) and other elite forces include this exercise in training.

Square lash (Fig Q)

This is used to secure one log at right angles to another log. It is useful for building shelters.

To tie, a clove hitch is tied around the log immediately under the place where the crosspiece will be located (1). In laying the turns, the rope goes on the

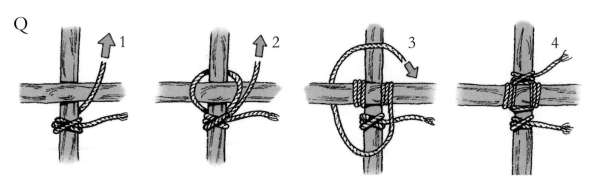

To make a square lashing secure, it is important to tighten each turn of the rope as it is made. Soldiers must take care not to chafe their hands when pulling the rope taught.

outside of the previous turn around the log (2). The rope should be kept tight. Three or four turns are necessary. The rope is then carried over and under both logs in an counterclockwise direction. Three or four circuits are made and then a full turn is made around a log and a circuit in the opposite direction (3). A soldier then finishes with a clove hitch around the same log that the lashing was started on (4).

Diagonal lash (Fig R)

Diagonal lashing is an alternative to square lashing, and is much more effective when the spars do not cross at right angles, or when the spars are under considerable strain and have to be pulled toward one another to be tied. It is a great strengthening device.

A clove hitch is tied around the two logs at the point of crossing. Three turns are taken around the two logs (1). The turns lie beside each other, not on top of each other. Three more turns are made around the two logs, this time crosswise over the previous turns. The turns must then be pulled tight.

Suited to both square and diagonal structure, diagonal lashings are essential for making temporary shelters and scaffolding.

Two frapping (diagonal) turns are made between the two logs, around the lashing turns (2). The lashing is finished with a clove hitch around the same pole the lash was started on (3).

Shear lash (Fig S)

Shear lashing is used for lashing together two or more logs. To tie, soldiers first place the desired number of logs side by side. They then start the lash with a clove hitch on the outer log (1). Logs are then lashed using seven or eight turns of the rope loosely laid beside each other (2). Frapping turns are made between each log (3). The lashing is finished with a full clove hitch on the log opposite to the first start log (4)

Making lashings from tendons and rawhide

The U.S. Army teaches its new recruits to make workable lashing material from a dead animal. **Tendons** and rawhide make excellent lashing materials.

TEXT-DEPENDENT QUESTIONS

1. List five examples of materials that can be used to create ropes? What is one advantage and one disadvantage of synthetic materials?
2. Explain what a "bight" is.
3. List six ways to take care of rope.
4. Why are synthetic ropes not suitable for square knots?
5. What are hitches used for?
6. What are two materials taken from dead animals that can be used to create ropes?

S

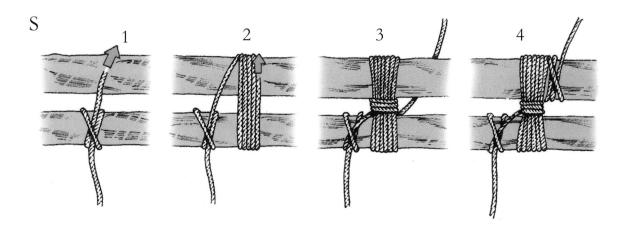

Shear lashing can be used to strengthen weak or broken poles. When made loosely, the poles can be opened out to create an A-frame, suitable for a temporary shelter.

RESEARCH PROJECT

Rope can be used to build all sorts of things, including bridges, weapons, and tools. Use the Internet or the library to research one item that can be made from rope. List the steps involved in the construction. Discuss what kinds of rope and which knots would be best suited for the project.

From tendons:

- They remove tendons from game the same day it is caught.

- They smash dried tendons into fibers.

- They moisten fibers and twist them into a continuous strand; the strands are braided if stronger lashing material is required.

From rawhide:

- They skin the animal and remove all fat and meat from the skin.

- They spread out skin and remove all folds.

- They cut skin into strips.

- They soak the strips in water for about two to four hours until soft and pliable.

WORDS TO UNDERSTAND

hostile: Unfriendly.

potential: The possibility of some future condition.

specialized: Focused on one particular thing.

USING ROPES IN THE MOUNTAINS

Mountains are hostile and dangerous. Freezing winds, driving snow, ice fields, mist, freezing fog, and heavy rainfall, are all potential killers. An elite soldier must learn how to survive them all. Ropes are a necessity, and troops are trained thoroughly in how to use them.

Knowledge of knots

It is vital that all soldiers have an excellent knowledge of the knots that they can use in mountainous terrain. There are a number of **specialized** knots for climbing. These are designed to have the least effect on the fiber of a rope lock without slipping, and to be easy to untie when conditions are wet and icy. Though all knots reduce the strength of ropes, these knots are designed to reduce their strength as little as possible. Most knots should be made safe with an overhand knot or two half hitches. (See previous chapter.) However, a knot does not have to be made safe if it is in the middle of a line.

Water knot

This knot, also called the ring bend, is used for joining nylon webbing, not rope.

For climbing and mountain rescue operations, soldiers use approved-quality ropes and equipment. A variety of rope colors is used for quick identification and checking of knots and attachments.

Figure-eight loop

The figure-eight loop can be tied at the end or in the middle of a line making
fixed loop. If the loop is tied at the end of the line, then an overhand or sing
fisherman's safety knot must be used.

Manharness hitch (Fig T)

Also called the butterfly or Alpine butterfly knot, it is used to make a fixed lo
in the middle of a line. A loop is made in the rope (1) and the left side of t
loop is allowed to cross over the loop (2). The loop is then twisted (3) befo
being passed over the left part of the rope and through the upper part of t
original loop (4). The knot is then pulled gently into shape and tightened (5).
a soldier does not twist the loop, the final strength of the loop does not app
to be reduced. The end result of not twisting the loop is shown in (6).

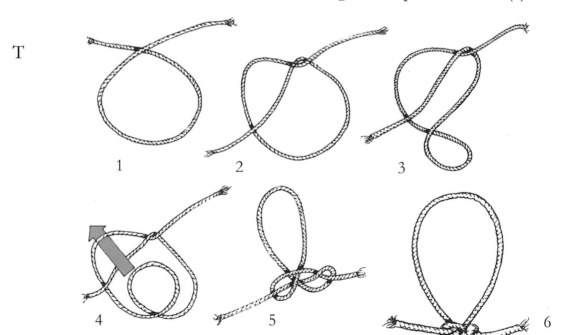

A manharness hitch is used as a harness to secure climbers between two othe
Strain can be applied to either side of this formation.

The person at the base of the mountain or cliff takes responsibility for feeding ropes upward and keeping ropes clear of each other.

MAKE CONNECTIONS: UPHILL AND DOWNHILL TRAVEL ACROSS SNOW

The soldiers of the British Special Air Service (SAS), like many elite units, are trained to fight in all types of terrain. Equipment, such as ropes, are particularly useful in mountainous terrains. Their rules for traveling up and down snow slopes on mountains are listed below.

- Use zigzag routes to traverse steep slopes; it is less stressful than a straight uphill climb.
- Always rope members of a team together for safety.
- In a team, change the lead person frequently. Since this person must choose the route of travel, he or she will get tired more quickly than the rest.
- When traversing a snow plain, use the heels and not the toes to form a step.
- When going downhill at speed, make sure all items of equipment, especially ice axes, are secured to backpacks.

Improvised seat harness

This can be made from nylon tape. The tape is placed across the back so that the end is on the hip opposite the hand that will be used for braking during belaying or the rappelling process. The midpoint is kept on the appropriate hip, the ends of the tape are crossed in front of the body, and three or four

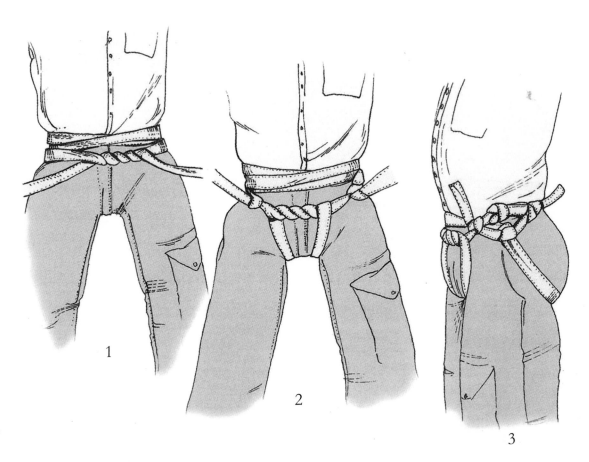

1

2

3

An improvised seat harness is used for transporting injured soldiers over ravines or river crossings. It is important to check the strength of the rope before it is allowed to take the weight of a human being.

overhand wraps are tied where the tapes cross (1). From front to rear, the ends of the tape are brought between the legs, around the legs, and are then secured with a hitch on both sides of the waist. The tapes are tightened by pulling down on the running ends to prevent them from crossing between the legs (2).

Both ends are brought around to the front and across the tape again. Then the tape is brought to the opposite side of the intended brake hand and a square knot is tied with an overhaul knot or two half-hitch safety knots on

An aluminum carrying harness is used by the U.S. Mountain Infantry Division during a simulated mountain rescue at Glacier National Park, Montana.

MAKE CONNECTIONS:
SWISS ALPINE CREVASSE RESCUE

Switzerland's mountain troops are well-known for their crevasse rescue skills. They have spent years mastering how to rescue climbers and survivors trapped in a crevasse. These are their rules for crevasse rescue:

- They pass a rope down with a loop in it. The suspended person can put a foot in it and therefore prevent the rope from accidentally catching his neck and choking him.

- It takes three people to haul an unconscious person out of a crevasse. Use the manharness hitches.

- Temperatures in crevasses are very low, so speed is vital.

either side of the square knot. (See previous chapter.) The safety knots should be passed around as much of the tape as possible (3). A soldier then clips a carabiner (coupling link with safety closure) to the harness by clipping together all the web around the waist and the web of the overhand wraps.

The use of belaying

Belaying is a rope technique used by two or more people to ascend a hill or mountain. One person (the climber) climbs up with a rope attached around the waist with a bowline, while the belayers secure the climb. The belayers anchor the rope with a loop tied in a figure-eight and tie on with a bight or two bights to steady themselves. They pass the climbing rope over the head and down to

Belaying lets the rope absorb slack should one of the climbers accidentally fall. Climbers used a combination of knots and bowline knots to ensure they are connected securely.

the hips, making a twist around the arm closest to the anchor, and take up the slack. The climber ties on with a bowline around the waist and will then start to ascend (A); the belayer takes in rope to avoid it becoming slack. It is important for the anchor belayer and climber to be in a straight line (B).

The sitting belay is the best position. The belayer sits and tries to get good bracing between the legs and buttocks. The legs should be straight, knees locked, with the rope running around the hips.

Procedure for belaying

U.S. Rangers, and other elite forces, are highly trained in belaying and rope work—they need to be able to break into enemy mountain positions quickly and efficiently.

- They run rope through a guiding knot and around the body.

- They anchor themselves to the rock with some of the climbing rope or a sling rope if their position is unsteady.

- They ensure the remainder of the rope is laid out so that it will run freely through the braking knot.

- They do not let too much slack develop and do not take up slack too suddenly—this could throw a climber off balance.

When descending, the climber keeps the rope loose enough to avoid friction around the hands and body.

- In the event of a fall, they relax the guiding hand, and let the rope slide enough so that the braking action is applied gradually. They then hold the belay position.

Troops are aware that walking rope will take a loading (breaking strain) of 2,000 pounds (907 kg), which is only just enough to save a person on a modest fall. A climber weighing 180 pounds (82 kg) falling 82 feet (24 m) will, when brought up, exert an equivalent force of 2,288 pounds (1,038 kg) on the rope. A rope intended to protect climbers against vertical falls should have a breaking strain of 4,200 pounds (1,900 kg). Failing this, troops use the double rope technique: two ropes together.

All climbers should be aware of the following dangers:

- Wet or icy rock—can make an easy route impossible.
- Snow—may cover holds.
- Smooth rock slabs—can be dangerous, especially if wet or icy.
- Rocks overgrown with moss or grass—dangerous when wet.
- Tufts of grass or small bushes—may be growing from loosely packed and unanchored soil.
- Talus slopes—can be dangerous because of falling rocks.
- Rock falls—frequently caused by other climbers, heavy rain, and extreme temperature changes in high mountains. In the event of a rock fall, troops seek shelter, or, if this is not possible, they lean into the slope to lessen the chance of being hit.
- Ridges—can be topped with unstable blocks.

The importance of rappelling

As long as elite soldiers have a rope, they can descend quickly by sliding down a rope that has been doubled around an anchor point. When rappelling, they will ensure that the rope reaches the bottom or a place from which further rappels can be made.

Troops carefully test the rappel point and inspect it to ensure the rope will run around it when one end is pulled from below. They also make sure that the area is clear of loose rocks; otherwise the rope may dislodge them during the

Wearing protective gloves, a U.S. Marine descends a rope (known as rappelling). Marines perform this maneuver from helicopters for both invasive operations and rescue missions.

Rapelling is more dangerous on steep, snowy, or ice-covered slopes, since there is an increased risk of surface movement and loss of balance.

rappel. If this happens, they may fall on persons below and inflict injuries. Soldiers face the anchor point and straddle the rope, then pull it from behind, run it around either hip, diagonally across the chest, and back over the opposite shoulder (A). From there, the rope runs to the braking hand, which is on the same side of the hip that the rope crosses. They must lean with the braking hand down and face slightly sideways (B). The foot on the same side as the braking hand should go before the other at all times.

Rappelling techniques

Italy's mountain troops, the Alpini, are among the most skilled alpine soldiers. These are their techniques for rappelling.

- They lean out at a 45-degree angle to the rock.
- They keep their legs well spread and straight for stability.
- They turn up their collars to prevent getting a rope burn on the back of the neck.
- They wear gloves and other articles of clothing to pad the hands, shoulders, and buttocks.

Protective clothing is essential to prevent injury and possible death. Helmets are compulsory, as are boots and safety harnesses.

- To brake, they lean back and face directly into the rock so that their feet are flat on the rock.
- They keep their feet shoulder width apart.

Anchoring climbing ropes

Some anchor systems are simple and consist of a single anchor point. Alternatively, they may be complex and made up of multiple anchor points. They provide protection for both the belayer and climber.

TEXT-DEPENDENT QUESTIONS

1. Explain what belaying and rappelling are.
2. Describe four kinds of natural anchoring points.
3. What are two kinds of artificial anchors?

The basis for any type of anchor is strong, secure points for attachment. Natural anchor points include the following: Chockstone—a natural chockstone is a securely wedged stone that provides an anchor point for a sling. In most cases, the rock is wedged within a crack.

Made from reinforced aluminium, carabiners are used to loop through one or more ropes, and as part of load-bearing knot formations.

RESEARCH PROJECT

When climbers are belaying, they use a special set of words and phrases to communicate. Use the Internet or library to find a list of these and explain what each means. Give examples of situations where each might be used.

Bollard—a rock bollard is a large rock or portion of rock that has an angular surface, over which a sling or rope can be placed so that it will not slip off. Troops must be careful to ensure that the bollard will not be pulled loose if it is subjected to a sudden load.

Tree—trees can make very secure anchor points, though in rocky or loose soil they should be avoided if other anchor points are available. If not, then troops must watch the tree very carefully for slippage.

Spike—a spike is a vertical projection of rock. To use as an anchor point, troops place a sling around the spike.

As well as natural anchors, elite soldiers use artificial anchors: chocks (metal wedges that fit into cracks) and pitons (metal spikes that can be driven into a crevice to secure a rope). They may consider using two or more anchor points, which will strengthen the whole anchor system. The drawback with this is that if one anchor fails, the remaining points will have to take a lot of strain.

WORDS TO UNDERSTAND

vegetation: Plants.

navigation: The process of finding out your location
and planning a route.

USING ROPES TO BUILD RAFTS

Troops need to be prepared for anything. They may find themselves having to escape being stranded on an island. It is vital that they know how to cope. If a soldier does have a rope, it will greatly aid him or her when building a raft. This may involve cutting it or even using it in one long piece. Raft-building is just another example of how useful ropes can be for an elite soldier.

Brush raft

This flotation device (see next page) will support around 253.5 pounds (115 kg) if made properly. Troops will need ponchos, fresh green brush, two small saplings, and a rope.

First, they tie off the neck of each poncho with the neck drawstring. They then attach the ropes at the corners and sides of each poncho and ensure they are long enough to tie with the rope on the opposite corner or side (A).

Second, they spread the poncho on the ground and pile fresh brush onto it until the stack is about 18 inches (45 cm) high. The poncho neck drawstring is then pulled up through the center of the stack. An X-frame is made of the two saplings and placed on top of the brush stack. The X-frame is tied securely in place with the poncho neck drawstring. Another 18 inches (45 cm) of brush is

A British SAS soldier inspects a raft during a survival exercise. Since the beams are attached at right angles, shear lashing is used to secure the structure. Floating is enabled by empty oil canisters.

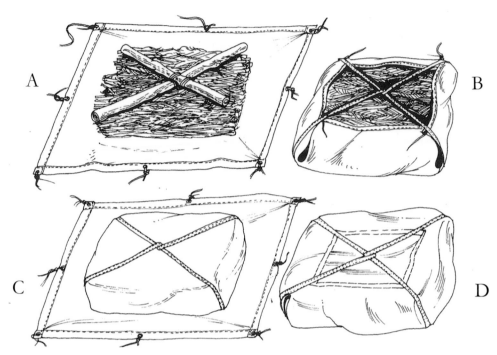

When assembling a brush raft, ensure that each corner is tied with equal tightness. The saplings must be young to ensure flexibility.

then piled on top of this. Third, the poncho sides are pulled up around the brush and the ropes are tied diagonally from corner to corner and from side to side (B). The second poncho is spread, tied-off hood up, next to the brush bundle.

Fourth, the brush bundle is rolled onto the center of the second poncho so that the tied side is down (C). The second poncho is tied around the brush bundle in the same way to tie the first poncho around the brush (D).

Vegetation raft

This raft is made out of small **vegetation** that will float. The plants, such as water hyacinth or cattail, are placed in material or clothing to form a raft for equipment or personnel. (It will not hold heavy weights, though.)

Log flotation

This is a simple flotation device for the single survivor (see below). It is made out of two logs of light wood. The logs are placed together about two feet (60 cm) apart, and are then tied together (A). A soldier will then be able to float on them (B).

Log raft

To make this raft, an elite soldier needs only logs, an axe, and a sheath knife. To carry three people, it should be 12 feet (3.6 m) long and six feet (1.8 m) wide. The logs themselves should have a diameter of 12 to 14 inches (30-35 cm).

Soldiers build the raft on two skid logs placed so that they slope down to the bank. They then smooth the logs with an axe and cuts two sets of notches, one

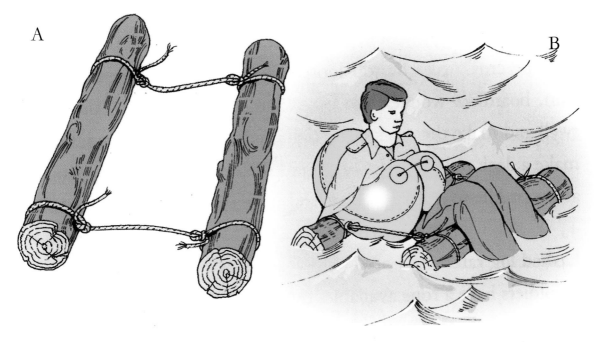

If wreckage materials are close to hand, a two-log raft can be made using a series of tight hitches. The survivor must take care to pull the knots taut.

TEXT-DEPENDENT QUESTIONS

1. List the steps for building a brush raft.
2. Which kind of raft requires two people to build it?
3. What are some possible hazards involved with rafting ashore?

in the top and bottom of both ends of each log. Once completed, they make the notches broader at the base than at the outer edge of the log. A three-sided wooden crosspiece one foot (30 cm) longer than the total width of the raft is driven through each end of the four sets of notches.

The soldiers then complete the notches on the tops of all the logs, turn them over, and drive a three-sided crosspiece through both sets of notches on the underside of the raft. After finishing the top set of notches, the soldiers drive the additional crosspieces through them. When the crosspieces are put in water, they will swell, resulting in the logs being tightly bound together.

If the crosspieces fit too loosely, soldiers can wedge them with thin, boardlike wooden pieces. When placed in water, the pieces swell and make the crosspieces tight and strong. Troops would then make a deck of light poles on top of the raft to keep equipment dry and a paddle to aid movement and **navigation**.

Lashed log raft

If soldiers have a rope available, they can construct a simple log raft (see opposite). They use pressure bars lashed securely at each end to hold the logs

RESEARCH PROJECT

Before you try to float your own raft, there are many safety rules you should take into consideration. Use the Internet or the library to find out what you need to do to be safe when using a raft. List these rules and explain how to follow them, even in emergency situations.

together. The building of this raft really requires two or more people because the gripper bars are under tension. Soldiers are very cautious if they have to make the raft on their own.

Warning on rafting ashore

Elite soldiers in one-person rafts will usually not have many problems making a shore landing. However, if the surf is strong, they could run the risk of capsizing. In this situation, they should sail around and look for a sandy, sloping beach where the surf is gentle.

Soldiers will not land when the sun is low and shining into their eyes, and they take care to avoid coral reefs and rocky cliffs. (Reefs do not occur near the mouths of freshwater streams.) They will not make a landing at night because they will not be able to see any dangers until it is too late. Members of one of the elite forces can use a traditional anchor to help them prevent the raft from capsizing, though they won't use it when traveling through coral. If the raft turns over in the surf, they must try to grab hold.

WORDS TO UNDERSTAND

insulating: Preventing the flow of heat from one thing to another.

superstructure: The framework above the base.

horizontally: Running from side to side, parallel to the ground.

projections: Things that stick out.

bipod: Something that has two-legged support.

alternately: Switching back and forth.

ventilation: Something that allows air to enter.

tension: Being stretched.

USING ROPES TO BUILD SHELTERS

Members of the elite forces need to be experts at building shelters. Troops always carry ropes in a survival situation because it is a great help in the task of making shelters.

Polar regions

Elite soldiers also need ropes for building shelter, which is an everyday task when living in the wilderness. Russia's deadly arctic warriors, Spetsnaz, are experts at fighting and surviving in the world's coldest regions. These are their tips for sheltering:

- Do not sleep on bare ground. Use **insulating** materials such as spruce or pine branches, dry grass, dried moss, or leaves.
- Do not cut wood that is oversized for a shelter; it uses valuable energy and requires more cord for lashings.
- **Superstructure** poles must be the largest and strongest; everything else rests on them.
- Do not scatter equipment on the ground; keep it in one place to avoid losing it.
- Have a fire going while building a shelter; it can be used as a heat source, a morale booster, and can provide boiling water to drink later.

Tight lashing is essential in windy or exposed regions. Posts must be secure to prevent the shelter blowing down.

An A-frame is an inverted V-shape, in which soldiers can sleep and/or keep watch on the enemy.

- Use clove hitches and finish with square knots for securing the structure.

A-frame shelter

This is a very simple shelter that can be constructed in a relatively short time. Elite soldiers will ensure their superstructure poles are strong enough to support the weight of the shelter materials. When constructing the framework, they will position the poles **horizontally** and cover them with boughs. They will then cover the shelter with snow and make a door plug.

To make this shelter, soldiers will need: one 12- to 18-foot (3.5–5.5-m) long sturdy ridge pole with all the branches and other **projections** cut off; two **bipod** poles approximately seven feet (2 m) long; materials to go over the A-frame or cut branches to form a framework; rope; and 14 stakes if they are going to use material over the A-frame.

Soldiers will lash the two bipod poles together at eye-level and place the ridge pole—with the large end on the ground—into the bipod formed by the poles and secure with a square lash. The bipod structure should be at a 90-degree angle to the ridge pole, with the bipod poles spread out to an approximate angle of about 60 degrees.

If they are using material to cover the A-frame, elite soldiers will use clove hitches and half hitches to secure the fabric to the front of the ridge pole. They will then stake down the fabric with the stakes, starting at the rear of the shelter and **alternately** staking from side to side to the front of the shelter. The stakes should be slanted or inclined away from the direction of pull. When soldiers are tying off with a clove hitch, the line should pass in front of the stake first and then pass under itself.

Pole preparation

When they are choosing poles for the framework, soldiers must ensure that all the rough edges and stubs have been removed. This will ensure that they will not get injured when they are crawling in and out. If they are using natural materials for the covering, they should use the shingle method. This requires them to start at the bottom and work toward the top of the shelter, with the bottom of each piece overlapping the top of the last piece: this will let water drain off. They take care to ensure that they use enough material to make a thick covering.

Lean-to shelter

This shelter is easy to make and can be both a summer or winter shelter. It will keep out insects, shield elite soldiers from rain and snow, and keep them warm. A fire should be built directly in front of it with a fire reflector on the other side to reflect heat back into the lean-to. When soldiers have built the framework, they cover it with boughs, starting from the bottom and working their way up with shingling, so that it overlaps. When they have constructed their shelter, they add a makeshift door, build a fire reflector, a porch, or a work/lookout area. They can even build another lean-to to face the first one they built if they have time.

Willow frame shelter

The willow frame shelter is very similar to the A-frame and lean-to shelters. Elite soldiers will build a framework as before, and then cover it from the bottom upward by simply overlapping the surface with tree branches. In winter, they can choose to cover the whole shelter with impacted layers of snow.

Sheltering in desert regions

Shelter is extremely important in the desert, both to protect soldiers from heat during the day and to keep them warm during the intense cold of the night. In flat, open deserts, natural shelters such as caves are hard to find. However,

A willow frame is similar to an A-frame. Troops cover it with boughs from the bottom up. It is commonly used in arctic conditions.

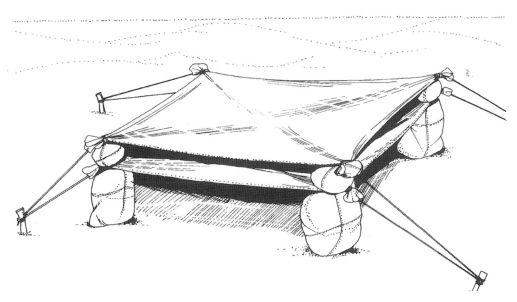

A simple desert shelter is open on all four sides to take advantage of any breeze during the day. The sides can be covered at night.

soldiers will gather together tumble weeds and mat them together. They will use any vegetation that they can find to make into a shelter.

Simple shelters

Troops are trained to build shelters that have more than one layer so that temperature in the shelter is reduced. Soldiers should place the floor of the shelter about 18 inches (45 cm) above or below the desert surface to increase the cooling effect. They will try to use a white material as the outer layer of the shelter, and the sides of the shelter should be movable to protect them during cold and windy periods and to provide **ventilation** in the extreme heat. Lastly, soldiers will build the shelter to take advantage of a breeze—it will keep them cool and keep insects away.

MAKE CONNECTIONS: BUILDING DESERT SHELTERS

Knowing when and where to build desert shelters can save you a lot of time and energy. Follow the advice of the French Foreign Legion, who are experts in desert survival:

- Build shelters during the early morning, late evening, or at night. It is less physically tiring.
- Build a shelter near fuel and water if possible.
- Do not build a shelter at the base of steep slopes or in areas where the soldier risks floods, rock falls, or battering by winds.
- Build shelters away from rocks that store up heat during the day. (Troops may wish to move to rocky areas during the night to take advantage of the warmth.)

Challenge of the tropics

In tropical jungles and rainforests, the ground is damp and full of insects, leeches, and reptiles. Troops must make a raised shelter that will let them sleep up off the ground. If they can, they build a shelter on a knoll or a high spot in a clearing well away from stagnant, still water.

There are a number of simple rules that troops follow when making shelters in the jungle. These rules, adopted by the Canadian Air Force for when they have crashed in enemy territory, help make them more comfortable.

- They never sleep on the ground; it may be damp and will certainly be crawling with insects.
- They make a bed by covering a pile of brush with layers of palm leaves or other broad leaves.
- They do not construct a shelter near a stream or pond, especially during the rainy season; it may get swept away.
- They do not build a shelter under dead trees or under a coconut tree. A falling coconut could kill you.

Banana leaf A-frame

This makes an excellent rain shelter. An elite soldier makes an A-type framework and shingles it with a good thickness of palm or other broad-leafed plants, with the leaves overlapping.

For surveillance and covert operations, troops may be equipped with shelter kits, including waterproof coverings and metal poles.

TEXT-DEPENDENT QUESTIONS

1. List the steps for making an A-frame structure.
2. Explain the shingle method.
3. Why do soldiers build structures with more than one layer?
4. Why is white used for the outer layers of desert structures?
5. List four things to avoid when building structures in tropical regions.
6. Why is it dangerous to camp under a coconut tree?

Raised platform shelters

These shelters have many variations. The poles are lashed together and crosspieces are then secured to form the platform on which material mattresses can be made. An elite soldier will try to make the roof waterproof with thatching laid from bottom to top in a thick shingle fashion. (It also helps to have a mosquito net.)

Troops can use split bamboo to make roofing. They cut the stem in half and lay them alternately to interlock with each other. They can also flatten split bamboo and use it for lining walls or shelving.

Hammock

A hammock can be made quickly if a soldier has a poncho or similar type of material and rope. A hammock may be tied between two trees or three or more for greater stability.

RESEARCH PROJECT

This chapter refers to different conditions in polar regions, deserts, and jungles. Use the Internet or library to locate and label these regions on a map of the world.

Materials for jungle shelters

Ropes are very useful for building a shelter, but troops also know there is an abundance of shelter-building material in the jungle. Troops know what it is and how to use it, but they will also be aware of its dangers.

- Atap, which has barbs at each leaf tip, is a vine that can be used to make shelters. Troops split each leaf from the tip and layer it on frames.
- Three-lobed leaves can be thatched on a frame.
- Elephant grass is large and can be woven on a frame.
- Bamboo can be used for pole supports, flooring, roofing, and walls.

Troops are careful when collecting bamboo; it grows in clusters and some stems are under **tension**. When disturbed, they can fly off and cause serious injury.

SERIES GLOSSARY
OF KEY TERMS

camouflage: Something that makes it hard to distinguish someone or something from the terrain or landscape around them.

casualty: A person who is killed or injured in a war or accident.

covert: Done in secret.

dehydrated: When you don't have enough water in your body for it to function properly. Alternatively, dehydrated food is food that has had all the water removed so that it won't go bad.

dislocation: When a joint is separated; when a bone comes out of its socket.

edible: Able to be eaten.

exposure: A health condition that results from bad weather around you. For example, when you get hypothermia or frostbite from cold weather, these are the results of exposure.

flares: A device that burns brightly, and can be used to signal for help. They can only be used once.

hygiene: The techniques and practices involved with keeping yourself clean and healthy.

improvised: Used whatever was available to make or create something. When you don't have professionally made equipment, you can make improvised equipment from the materials naturally found around you.

insulation: Something that keeps you warm and protects you from the cold.

kit: All of the clothing and equipment carried by a soldier.

layering: A technique of dressing for the wilderness that involves wearing many layers of clothing. If you become too warm or too cold, it is easy to remove or add a layer.

marine: Having to do with the ocean.

morale: Confidence, enthusiasm, and discipline at any given time. When morale is high, you are emotionally prepared to do something difficult. When morale is low, you might be angry, scared, or anxious.

purification: The process of making water clean and safe enough to drink.

terrain: The physical features of a stretch of land. Hard or rough terrain might be mountains or thick forests, and easy terrain would be an open field.

windbreak: Something that you use to block the wind from hitting you. If you camp somewhere exposed to the wind, it will be very difficult to stay warm.

EQUIPMENT REQUIREMENTS

Clothing and shelter

Thermal underwear

Thin layer of synthetic material

Woolen or wool mixture shirt

Woven fiber sweater or jacket (normally a fleece)

Waterproof and windproof final layer

Two pairs of socks (minimum)

Compact, light, windproof pants with numerous pockets with zippers, to carry items securely

Waterproof pants

Gloves—leather or mittens

Balaclava (woolen hat that covers face and neck)

Spare clothing—socks, underwear, shirts, etc.

Soft, well-maintained leather boots

H-frame bergen (backpack) with side pockets

Portable, lightweight, waterproof shelter

Survival tin

Knife

Matches

Flint

Sewing kit

Water purification tablets

Compass

Mirror

Safety pins

Wire

Plastic bag

Antiseptic cream

Snare wire

Survival bag

Pliers with wire cutter

Dental floss (for sewing)

Folding knife

Ring saw

Snow shovel

Signal cloth

Fishing hooks and flies

Weights and line

Multivitamins

Protein tablets

Large chocolate bar

Dried eggs

Dried milk

File

Cutlery set
Three space blankets
Four candles
Microlite flashlight
Extra battery and bulb
Fire starter
Windproof and waterproof matches
Butane lighter
Insect repellent
Snares
Plastic cup
Slingshot and ammunition
Knife sharpener
Whistle
Soap
Two orange smoke signals
Mess tin

EQUIPMENT FOR HOSTILE TERRAINS

Polar regions

Waterproof and windproof layers
Many inner layers of clothing for insulation
Goggles
Three layers of socks
Waterproof canvas boots
Ice axe
Ski stick
Rope

Desert

Light-colored clothing (reflects sunlight)
Cloth neckpiece
Sunglasses or goggles

Tropical regions

Talcum powder
Insect repellent
Machete
Hammock
Mosquito netting
Tropical medicines

USEFUL WEBSITES

www.wilderness-survival.net/shelters-2.php
www.usscouts.org
www.backpacker.com/skills-slideshow-series-learn-how-to-tie-knots/skills/14365
www.realknots.com
www.scouts.ca

FURTHER READING

Budworth, Geoffrey. *The Ultimate Book of Everyday Knots.* New York: Skyhorse Publishing, 2012.

Hopkins, Richard. Knots. San Diego, Calif.: Thunder Bay Press, 2003.

Luebben, Craig. *How to Rappel!* Guilford, Conn.: Falcon Publishing Company, 2002.

Pawson, Des. *Knots: The Complete Visual Guide.* New York: DK Publishing, 2012.

Wilderness Education Association. *Rock Climbing.* Champaign, Ill.: Human Kinetics, 2009.

ABOUT THE AUTHOR

Patrick Wilson was educated at Marlborough College, Wiltshire and studied history at Manchester University. He was a member of the Officer Training Corps, and for the past seven years he has been heavily involved in training young people in the art of survival on Combined Cadet Force (CCF) and Duke of Edinburgh Courses. He has taught history at St. Edward's School, Oxford, Millfield School, and currently at Bradfield College in England.

His main passion is military history. His first book was *Dunkirk—From Disaster to Deliverance* (Pen & Sword, 2000). Since then he has written *The War Behind the Wire* (Pen & Sword, 2000), which accompanied a television documentary on prisoners of war. He recently edited the diaries of an Australian teenager in the First World War.

INDEX